Defining MOMENTS

Cesar CHAVEZ

We Can Do It!

by Sunita Apte

CONSULTANT
Lynn D. Gordon
Associate Professor of History
University of Rochester

BEARPORT
PUBLISHING COMPANY, INC.
New York, New York

Credits
Cover, Tim Graham/Evening Standard/Getty Images; Title page, Arthur Schatz/
Time Life Pictures/Getty Images; 4–5 (both), © 1976 George Ballis/Take Stock;
6, AP/Wide World Photos; 7, Library of Congress Prints and Photographs Division
Washington, DC; 8–9 (both), Library of Congress Prints and Photographs Division
Washington, DC; 10, ™/© 2005 the Cesar E. Chavez Foundation; 11 (both),
Library of Congress Prints and Photographs Division Washington, DC; 12, ™/©
2005 the Cesar E. Chavez Foundation; 13, © 1976 George Ballis/Take Stock;
14, ™/© 2005 the Cesar E. Chavez Foundation; 15, Library of Congress Prints and
Photographs Division Washington, DC; 16, ™/© 2005 the Cesar E. Chavez
Foundation; 17, Walter P. Reuther Library, College of Urban, Labor and
Metropolitan Affairs, Wayne State University, Detroit; 18, Walter P. Reuther
Library, College of Urban, Labor and Metropolitan Affairs, Wayne State
University, Detroit; 19, Walter P. Reuther Library, College of Urban, Labor and
Metropolitan Affairs, Wayne State University, Detroit; 20, © 1976 George Ballis/
Take Stock; 21, AP/Wide World Photos; 22–23 (both), © 1976 George Ballis/Take
Stock; 24, © 1976 George Ballis/Take Stock; 25, Bob Parent/Hulton Archive/Getty
Images; 26, AP/Wide World Photos/Greg Gibson; 27, AP/Wide World Photos/
Damian Dovarganes.

Editorial development by Judy Nayer
Design by Fabia Wargin; Production by Luis Leon; Image Research by Jennifer Bright

Library of Congress Cataloging-in-Publication Data
Apte, Sunita.
  Cesar Chavez : we can do it! / by Sunita Apte.
    p. cm. — (Defining moments)
  Includes bibliographical references and index.
  ISBN 1-59716-073-3 (library binding) — ISBN 1-59716-110-1 (pbk.)
  1. Chavez, Cesar, 1927—Juvenile literature. 2. Labor leaders—United States—
Biography—Juvenile literature. 3. Mexican American migrant agricultural
laborers—Biography—Juvenile literature. 4. United Farm Workers—History—
Juvenile literature. I. Title. II. Series: Defining moments (Bearport Publishing).

  HD6509.C48A685 2006
  331.88'13'092—dc22

                              2005005220

For more information, write to Bearport Publishing Company, Inc.,
101 Fifth Avenue, Suite 6R, New York, New York 10003.
Printed in the United States of America.

1 2 3 4 5 6 7 8 9 10

Table of Contents

A Man of Hope

It was April 10, 1966. More than 10,000 people were gathered in Sacramento, the capital city of California. Most of them were Mexican-American farm workers. These workers **toiled** in fields all day, picking grapes, cotton, or other crops. The work was hard. Their lives were hard.

Cesar Chavez believed that **nonviolent protest** was the best way to bring about change. Instead of fighting, he led a peaceful march to help farm workers.

Cesar's movement to make life better for farm workers was known as la causa, or the cause.

The farm workers had come to see one man. He was a Mexican American who gave them hope. His name was Cesar Chavez (SAY-zar SHA-vez). Cesar had walked 340 miles (547 km) to Sacramento. It took him almost a month. He had walked to draw attention to the lives of farm workers. Now, the entire nation was paying attention.

A Hard Life

Cesar Chavez knew about the farm worker's life. He had been a **migrant** farm worker for many years. He had moved from place to place to find work, picking crops. He had spent long hours in the hot sun. He had bent down all day, working in the fields.

Migrant workers spent ten or twelve hours a day laboring in the hot sun.

Migrant workers had to live in dirty, run-down shacks or tents. Some even lived under bridges. They didn't have bathrooms or running water.

Farm workers weren't paid much for all their hard work. Often, the growers they worked for cheated them. Most farm workers made barely enough to live. To survive, the whole family had to work in the fields, including the children. Cesar had been working in the fields since he was 11 years old.

Yuma

Cesar's life hadn't always been so hard. He was born near Yuma (YOO-mah), Arizona, in 1927. His family owned a small store and a farm. They were not rich, but life was good.

Then the **Great Depression** hit. People lost their jobs and had no money. No one could afford to shop at the store. Cesar's parents had to sell it.

The Great Depression was a period of extreme hardship. Many people lost their jobs and didn't have enough to eat. Here, people wait in line for free meals.

After losing their farm, the Chavez family joined 300,000 migrant workers who traveled the state of California picking crops for farm owners.

During the Great Depression a terrible **drought** struck many states. It lasted for years. The river that watered the Chavez family farm eventually dried up.

The family struggled to survive. Soon, however, they lost the farm. At that point, they decided to leave Arizona and drive to California to look for work.

Cesar's grandfather, Cesario, first worked the land that became the Chavez family farm. He came to Arizona from Mexico in 1888.

"No Dogs or Mexicans Allowed"

Cesar's father often had trouble finding work in California. Sometimes, he would hear about a farm job. The family would drive long hours to get to the farm. When they arrived, there would be no job, or the job paid much less than the family had hoped.

Cesar with his family

The Chavez family also faced **discrimination**. Many white Californians looked down on Mexican Americans. Some restaurants had signs that read, "No Dogs or Mexicans Allowed." Mexican Americans were even supposed to sit in a special section at the movie theater.

The Chavez family saw many signs like this one.

From School to the Fields

Cesar's family finally settled in a poor neighborhood near San Jose (SAN HOH-zay), California. The neighborhood was called *Sal Si Puedes,* or "Get Out If You Can."

When Cesar was 15 years old, his father was hurt in a car accident. Instead of going to high school, Cesar had to work in the fields. It was the only way his family could survive.

School wasn't always a happy place for Cesar. Mexican-American students were punished for speaking Spanish at school.

Farm work was grueling. Cesar's back ached from bending down all day. His eyes stung from the chemicals sprayed in the fields to kill insects. His skin tore from yanking out beets. He had no rest breaks, no bathrooms, and no clean water to drink.

Cesar's family constantly traveled around California to work in the fields. Cesar attended 37 schools before he was 15 years old.

Cesar lived in a California neighborhood similar to this one.

"Why Can't I Sit Where I Want to Sit?"

Cesar wanted to go back to school. Instead, however, he joined the U.S. Navy.

Cesar hated the discrimination he experienced in the Navy. He felt that white people did not treat Mexican Americans fairly.

Cesar in the Navy

In the 1950s, movie theaters in many parts of the country had sections reserved for "Whites Only."

All the **injustice** made Cesar angry. Once, when he was home on leave, Cesar went to the movies. He sat in the white section of the theater and refused to move. The police came and took Cesar to the station.

After a while, the police let Cesar go. He was still angry, though. Cesar knew the rules were unfair, but he wasn't sure how to change them.

The Chance to Change Things

When Cesar got out of the Navy, he married Helen Fabela. Together, they worked in the fields. Cesar's time in the Navy had convinced him that Mexican-American farm workers needed to demand better treatment.

Cesar first met Helen when they were both only 15 years old.

Cesar and Helen taught Mexican Americans to read and write so they could take the test to become American **citizens**.

Cesar talked to other farm workers about fighting for change. He listened to their problems. He became known around his neighborhood as someone worth talking to.

Fred Ross heard about Cesar from a friend. Ross ran the Community Service Organization, or CSO. The CSO worked to help poor Mexican Americans. Ross hired Cesar. At last, Cesar would have a chance to change things.

After meeting Cesar for the first time, Fred Ross wrote in his journal, "I think I've found the guy I'm looking for."

The Start of Something Big

Cesar helped many people during his ten years at the CSO. Still, he thought that farm workers needed to form their own group to demand fair treatment. They needed a **union**.

In 1962, Cesar quit the CSO to start the National Farm Workers Association, or NFWA. He wasn't sure it would be a success. To his surprise, many farm workers quickly joined the union. They were ready to fight for their rights.

Cesar's brother, Richard, helped design the union's flag.
The black eagle was the sacred bird of the Aztec Indians.

At its first convention, the NFWA picked its motto:
"¡Viva la causa!" or "Long live the cause!"

The first big fight came three years later. In 1965, the union went on **strike** against some grape growers in Delano (di-LAY-noh), California. Union members stopped work and demanded better pay.

In 1962, farm workers had the longest hours, lowest pay, and harshest conditions of any group of workers in America. Just before the 1965 strike, grape growers cut their pay even more.

"Don't Buy Grapes!"

Day after day, workers **picketed** grape farms. They marched up and down, shouting *"¡Huelga!"* (WEL-gah) or "Strike!"

The growers didn't give in. They thought the farm workers would run out of money. Then the workers would have to come back to their jobs.

In the 1960s, grape **boycotts** cost California grape growers more than $25 million.

In Delano, the strikers were treated very poorly. The police often arrested and beat them.

Union organizers went all over the country with the message "Don't buy grapes!" Many Americans supported the boycott.

Cesar wanted to put pressure on the growers. He needed the rest of America to support the strike. He sent union workers to cities across the United States. They went to supermarkets and told people, "Don't buy grapes."

The growers lost a lot of money because of the boycott. Still, they didn't give in.

Marching to Victory

Cesar decided that something more was needed to grab the public's attention. So, he organized a march with 67 other protestors. He began walking the 340 miles (547 km) from Delano to Sacramento on March 17, 1966. The marchers carried banners reading *"¡Viva la causa!"* Each day, more people joined the march.

Reporters and film crews followed the marchers. They learned how farm workers lived. They saw the migrant shacks. They shared the truth with people everywhere.

The walk to Sacramento was the longest protest march in U.S. history.

During the march, Cesar's ankles swelled and his feet became covered in blisters. He had to use a cane to walk.

The growers didn't like the **publicity**. Finally, they agreed to the union's demands. On the steps of Sacramento's capitol building, Cesar joyously announced the victory.

The Fight Goes On

Cesar didn't stop his protests. There were plenty of other grape growers in Delano. He knew the union needed to fight them, too.

Cesar continued the fight. It took four more years. Finally, in 1970, the rest of Delano's grape growers signed **contracts** with the union.

By 1968, the grape strike had been going on for three years. Cesar wanted people to know that he wasn't giving up. So he began a **fast**. He didn't eat for 25 days.

Senator Robert Kennedy (left) helps Cesar celebrate the end of his fast.

Then Cesar turned his attention to California's lettuce growers. He organized strikes and boycotts against them. He was sent to jail for his work. In the end, however, his union won.

In 1975, California passed the Agricultural Labor Relations Act. This law promised basic rights for all farm workers.

Coretta Scott King, wife of Martin Luther King, Jr., and Cesar leading a lettuce boycott march in New York City in 1973

A True Friend of Farm Workers

Cesar Chavez died in 1993, at the age of 66. Fifty-thousand people came to his funeral.

Helen Chavez receives the Presidential Medal of Freedom in her husband's honor from President Bill Clinton.

In 1994, a year after he died, Cesar Chavez was awarded the Presidential Medal of Freedom. He was only the second Mexican American to receive this honor.

Members of Cesar's family march with others in honor of the 10th anniversary of his death in 2003.

For over 30 years, Cesar had fought for a better life for farm workers. He had starved himself, marched hundreds of miles, spent time in jail, and even received death **threats**.

Through it all, Cesar never lost hope. He never stopped believing that change was possible. *"¡Sí, se puede!"* he said. "Yes, it can be done." Cesar proved that poor people could fight and win. He had done it.

Just the Facts

■ Cesar and Helen had eight children: Fernando, Sylvia, Linda, Anna, Eloise, Paul, Elizabeth, and Anthony.

■ In 1966, at the time of Cesar's march, the average farm worker earned just $2,400 a year.

■ Cesar's union, NFWA, became part of a bigger, national group of unions that was called the United Farm Workers of America, AFL-CIO, also known as the UFW.

Timeline

Here are some important events in the life of Cesar Chavez.

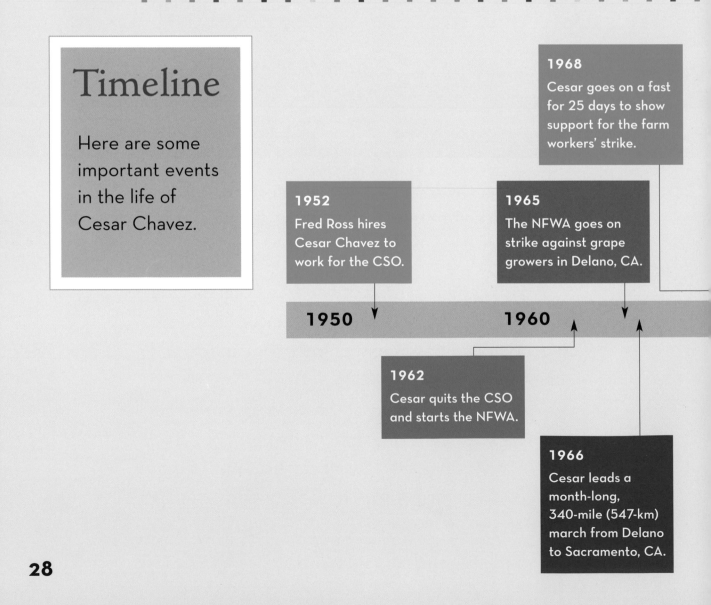

1968
Cesar goes on a fast for 25 days to show support for the farm workers' strike.

1952
Fred Ross hires Cesar Chavez to work for the CSO.

1965
The NFWA goes on strike against grape growers in Delano, CA.

1950

1960

1962
Cesar quits the CSO and starts the NFWA.

1966
Cesar leads a month-long, 340-mile (547-km) march from Delano to Sacramento, CA.

■ The UFW didn't just support farm workers in California. In 1972, the union reached a deal with Coca-Cola to improve the lives of migrant workers in Florida.

■ After his 1968 fast, Cesar went on two more hunger strikes. In 1972, he stopped eating for 24 days. In 1988, he stopped eating for 36 days.

■ Cesar won many fights for better wages and working conditions, including the banning of the short-handled hoe. This tool had caused major back injuries to thousands of workers.

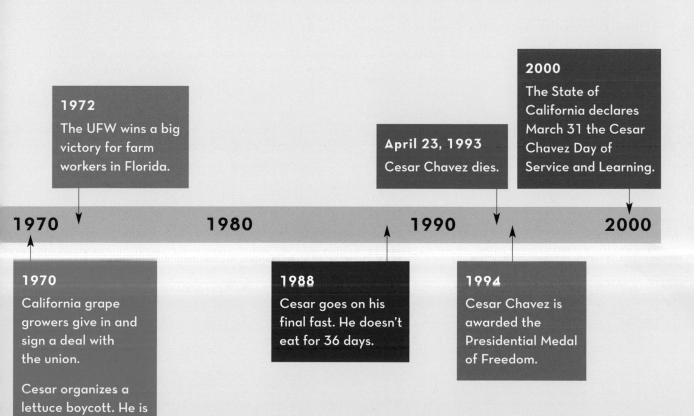

1972
The UFW wins a big victory for farm workers in Florida.

April 23, 1993
Cesar Chavez dies.

2000
The State of California declares March 31 the Cesar Chavez Day of Service and Learning.

1970   **1980**   **1990**   **2000**

1970
California grape growers give in and sign a deal with the union.

Cesar organizes a lettuce boycott. He is jailed for three weeks.

1988
Cesar goes on his final fast. He doesn't eat for 36 days.

1994
Cesar Chavez is awarded the Presidential Medal of Freedom.

Glossary

boycotts (BOI-kots) acts of refusing to buy or use something in order to make a protest

citizens (SIT-i-zuhnz) members of a certain country who have the right to live there

contracts (KON-trakts) agreements under the law

discrimination (*diss*-krim-i-NAY-shuhn) the unfair treatment of people because of their race or background

drought (DROUT) a long period with little or no rain

fast (FAST) not eating for a period of time

Great Depression (GRAYT di-PRESH-uhn) a period in the 1930s when many people in the United States lost their jobs and were very poor

injustice (in-JUHSS-tiss) unfair treatment of people

migrant (MYE-gruhnt) moving from place to place to find work

nonviolent protest (*non*-VYE-uh-luhnt PROH-test) demonstrating against something without causing any harm, such as through peaceful marches and strikes

picketed (PIK-it-id) marched outside a workplace to show others that a strike is taking place

publicity (puh-BLISS-uh-tee) information given out through TV and other media that gets the attention of many people

strike (STRIKE) refusing to work until pay and other conditions asked for are agreed upon

threats (THRETS) warnings that punishment or harm will happen

toiled (TOI-uhld) worked extremely hard

union (YOON-yuhn) a group that works to make people's jobs better

Bibliography

Ferriss, Susan, and Ricardo Sandoval. *The Fight in the Fields.* Orlando, FL: Paradigm Productions, Inc. (1997).

Jensen, Richard J., and John C. Hammerback, eds. *The Words of Cesar Chavez.* College Station, Texas: Texas A&M University Press (2002).

Matthiessen, Peter. *Sal Si Puedes (Escape If You Can): Cesar Chavez and the New American Revolution.* Berkeley, CA: University of California Press (2000).

Rodriguez, Consuelo. *Cesar Chavez.* New York: Macmillan/McGraw-Hill (1991).

Read More

Collins, David R. *Farmworker's Friend: The Story of Cesar Chavez.* Minneapolis, MN: Carolrhoda Books (1996).

deRuiz, Dana Catherine. *La Causa: The Migrant Farmworkers' Story.* Austin, TX: Steck-Vaughn (1992).

Gonzales, Doreen. *Cesar Chavez: Leader for Migrant Farm Workers.* Springfield, NJ: Enslow Publishers (1996).

Krull, Kathleen. *Harvesting Hope: The Story of Cesar Chavez.* San Diego, CA: Harcourt, Inc. (2003).

Soto, Gary. *Cesar Chavez: A Hero for Everyone.* New York: Aladdin Paperbacks (2003).

Zannos, Susan. *Cesar Chavez: A Real-Life Reader Biography.* Hockessin, DE: Mitchell Lane Publishers (1998).

Learn More Online

Visit these Web sites to learn more about Cesar Chavez:

www.cesarechavezfoundation.org
www.sfsu.edu/~cecipp/cesar_chavez/chavezhome.htm
www.ufw.org

Index

About the Author

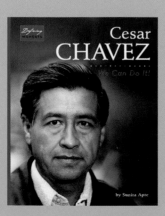

SUNITA APTE is a children's book author living in Brooklyn, New York. When she's not writing books for kids, she likes to cook and travel the world.